> RECIPE OF THE WEEK ···· COOKIES ····

▶ RECIPE OF THE WEEK

COOKIES

● ● ● ● ● ● ● ● 52 EASY RECIPES FOR
YEAR-ROUND BAKING

SALLY SAMPSON

PHOTOGRAPHY BY YUNHEE KIM

BICENTENNIAL
1807
WILEY
2007
BICENTENNIAL

JOHN WILEY & SONS, INC.

Published by John Wiley & Sons, Inc., Hoboken, New Jersey
Published simultaneously in Canada

For general information about our other products and services, please contact our Customer Care Department within the United States at (800) 762-2974, outside the United States at (317) 572-3993 or fax (317) 572-4002. Wiley also publishes its books in a variety of electronic formats. Some content that appears in print may not be available in electronic books. For more information about Wiley products, visit our web site at www.wiley.com.

BOOK DESIGN BY DEBORAH KERNER DESIGN
PHOTOGRAPHY COPYRIGHT © 2007 BY YUNHEE KIM
FOOD STYLING BY JEE LEVIN
PROP STYLING BY DEBORAH WILLIAMS

Library of Congress Cataloging-in-Publication Data:

Sampson, Sally, 1955-
    Recipe of the week : cookies / Sally Sampson.
        p. cm.
    ISBN 13: 978-0-471-92190-5 (pbk.)
    1. Cookies. I. Title.
    TX772.S22 2006
    641.8'654--dc22

                                    2006027911

Printed in China
10 9 8 7 6 5 4 3 2

For **Lauren** and **Ben**,

who are *almost* sick of cookies.

Contents

Acknowledgments   **ix**

Introduction   **x**

Essential Ingredients   **xii**

Essential Equipment   **xiii**

the recipes   1

List of Recipe Titles by the Week   **86**

Index   **93**

Acknowledgments

I *really* wouldn't have so thoroughly enjoyed or been able to complete this book without the help of many eager eaters (and critics): primarily Lauren's eighth-grade class at Cambridge Friends School and Ben's sixth-grade class at Watertown Middle School. My most enthusiastic, indispensable and faithful pal, recipe tester and taster was Nancy Olin. Zach Demuth helped with research but amazingly, never even got to eat one cookie. And of course Justin Schwartz, my editor, who raved about the cookies and made the book cohesive and beautiful, and Carla Glasser, my most beloved agent and friend.

There would be no pleasure to such a book without each of them.

introduction

A few weeks after starting this book, I noticed, not surprisingly, that I had gained some weight. When I complained to my friend Donna, she blithely suggested that when I test new recipes, I simply take a bite and toss the remaining cookie.

Now, clearly, this advice comes from someone with inhuman willpower. So when I complained to my friend and agent Carla, who is more realistic, I felt her words had actual substance: "Sally," she said, "if you can stop before you eat six, the cookie just isn't good enough to be in this book." Now that's levelheaded. I ate one when the cookie was hot and gooey, then another when it was warm but not gooey. Yet another when completely cooled. One with tea, one with milk and one, later, frozen. You get the idea. The truth is: **these cookies, each and every one, are enough to weaken any resolve.**

If you aren't on a deadline, making one cookie each week is a very attainable goal. Whether you have young children around or want to be very popular with older ones; are hosting tea parties, bake sales or dinner parties; or just want to be a cookie connoisseur; these recipes take little time to prepare and bake and are straightforward, ageless, absolutely delicious and completely irresistible.

Bet you can't eat just one.

Essential Ingredients

All-purpose flour

Quick-cooking or old-fashioned oats

White sugar

Light brown sugar

Dark brown sugar

Confectioners' sugar

Baking soda

Baking powder

Kosher salt

Ground ginger

Ground cinnamon

Ground nutmeg

Unsweetened cocoa powder

Blackstrap molasses

Vanilla extract

Peanut butter

Unsalted butter

Assorted nuts, especially pecans, walnuts and almonds

Semi-sweet chocolate chips

Large eggs

Essential Equipment

18 x 12 rimless cookie sheet

Stand mixer with paddle

Food processor

Rubber spatula

Offset spatula (the kind where the metal bends where it meets the handle), the absolute essential kind for lifting cookies off the cookie sheet

Wooden spoons

Assorted metal, glass or ceramic mixing bowls

Stainless steel measuring cups

Stainless steel measuring spoons

Cookie scoops (ice cream scoops), assorted sizes

Wire cooling racks

Acrylic or wood cutting board

Kitchen timer

Silpat/Exopat (two different brand names) are flexible, non-stick silicone baking mats that can be used instead of parchment or wax paper. The manufacturers claim you can get 2,000–3,000 uses out of each mat but I actually think you get more. At $20–$30 each they don't seem inexpensive, but if you bake cookies a lot they are invaluable.

Parchment or wax paper

the recipes

Gingersnaps

Gingersnaps are among my most beloved cookies; the subtle but real heat of the ginger, here both fresh and ground, makes this cookie more sophisticated than most. It's especially pleasing served with vanilla ice cream or mango sorbet.

½ cup (¼ pound/1 stick) unsalted butter, at room temperature

¾ cup plus 2 tablespoons sugar

1 large egg, at room temperature

3 tablespoons dark molasses

1 tablespoon peeled and finely chopped fresh ginger root

2 cups all-purpose white flour

1 tablespoon ground ginger

1½ teaspoons baking soda

½ teaspoon ground cinnamon

¼ teaspoon kosher salt

FOR THE GINGER SUGAR:

3 tablespoons white sugar

¾ teaspoon ground ginger

Preheat the oven to 350°F. Line a cookie sheet with parchment paper.

Place the butter and sugar in the bowl of a mixer fitted with the paddle attachment and mix until smooth and creamy. Scrape down the sides of the bowl, add the egg and molasses, one at a time, mixing well between additions. Scrape down the sides of the bowl, add the remaining ingredients and mix until everything is well incorporated. Scrape down the sides of the bowl and mix again.

To make the ginger sugar: Place the sugar and ginger on a plate and mix until well incorporated. Set aside.

To form the cookies: Break off small pieces and roll into 1-inch balls. Roll the balls in the ginger sugar and place 2 inches apart on the prepared cookie sheet. Using your hand or the bottom of a water glass, press down until flattened. Alternatively, you can roll the dough into a log (see page 4). Transfer to the oven and bake until the cookies begin to brown at the edges, 12 to 15 minutes. Cool on the cookie sheet. Transfer the cookies to a wire rack and repeat with the remaining dough.

Cookie Logs

To prepare cookies using the log method, roll the dough into one or two 1- to 2-inch cylinders, depending upon the cookie, and cover with parchment paper. Either place the cylinders into a resealable plastic bag or cover with plastic wrap. Refrigerate about 20 minutes and then reform the cylinder to ensure that the shape is uniform. Continue to refrigerate until the dough is firm, at least 1 hour and up to 2 days. When ready to bake, slice the cylinder into rounds, $1/8$ to $1/2$ inch thick, depending upon the cookie. If desired, you can freeze the dough for 1 month.

Ben's Molasses Cookies

Spicier and less ginger-y but somewhat like a gingersnap, this cookie has been my son Ben's favorite since he was 2 years old.

Molasses, the byproduct of cane sugar processing, imparts a great, albeit slightly bitter, flavor to cookies. There are three grades of molasses: the higher the grade, the more bitter tasting the molasses. The third, and final, grade is known as blackstrap molasses because of its deep brown, almost black, color.

¾ cup (1½ sticks) unsalted butter, at room temperature

1 cup white sugar, plus additional for rolling

1 large egg, at room temperature

¼ cup blackstrap molasses

1 teaspoon vanilla extract

2 cups all-purpose white flour

2 teaspoons baking soda

1 teaspoon ground cinnamon

½ teaspoon ground cardamom

½ teaspoon ground ginger

½ teaspoon kosher salt

Preheat the oven to 375°F. Line a cookie sheet with parchment paper.

Place the butter and sugar in the bowl of a mixer fitted with the paddle attachment and mix until smooth and creamy. Scrape down the sides of the bowl, add the egg, molasses and vanilla, one at a time, mixing well between additions. Scrape down the sides of the bowl, add the remaining ingredients and mix until everything is well incorporated. Scrape down the sides of the bowl and mix again.

To form the cookies: break off small pieces and roll into 1-inch balls. Roll the balls in the sugar and place 2 inches apart on the prepared cookie sheet. Using your hand or the bottom of a water glass, press down until flattened. Alternatively, you can roll the dough into a log (see page 4). Transfer to the oven and bake until the cookies begin to brown at the edges, 12 to 15 minutes. Cool on the cookie sheet. Transfer to a wire rack and repeat with the remaining dough.

Amanda Hewell's Coffee Crisps

Amanda Hewell, the sister of my friend Adam Reid, originally got this recipe from a California Culinary Academy cookbook. She adapted it (by putting a mocha bean candy in the middle), gave it to Adam, who transcribed it incorrectly and gave it to me. I then read it too quickly and ended up making some changes myself (by adding the chocolate chips and the chocolate nibs). This is a perfect case of a recipe that has morphed and morphed into something absolutely amazing.

Mocha bean candies are not chocolate covered coffee beans. They are glossy little solid chocolate candies, about the size and shape of coffee beans and with a distinct coffee flavor. Cocoa nibs are roasted, shelled cocoa beans.

¾ cup (1½ sticks) unsalted butter, at room temperature

½ cup plus 3 tablespoons white sugar

½ cup light brown sugar

1 tablespoon powdered or granulated instant coffee or finely ground coffee beans

1 large egg yolk, at room temperature

1½ teaspoons vanilla extract

1¾ cups all-purpose white flour

¼ teaspoon baking soda

¼ teaspoon baking powder

¼ teaspoon kosher salt

½ cup (3 ounces) semi-sweet chocolate chips

½ cup cocoa nibs

½ cup mocha bean candies (optional)

Place the butter, sugars and powdered coffee in the bowl of a mixer fitted with the paddle attachment and mix until smooth and creamy. Scrape down the sides of the bowl, add the egg yolk and vanilla, one at a time, mixing well between additions. Scrape down the sides of the bowl, add the flour, baking soda, baking powder and salt and mix until everything is well incorporated. Scrape down the sides of the bowl, add the chocolate chips and nibs and mix again.

Divide the dough into quarters, roll each section into a 1½-inch-wide log, wrap with parchment or wax paper and refrigerate for at least 1 hour and up to 2 days.

Preheat the oven to 375°F. Line a cookie sheet with parchment paper.

Cut the dough logs into ¼-inch-thick slices and place the slices 2 inches apart on the prepared cookie sheet. Press one mocha bean candy in the center of each slice, if desired. Transfer to the oven and bake until the cookies begin to brown at the edges, 11 to 12 minutes. Cool on the cookie sheet. Transfer to a wire rack and repeat with the remaining dough.

Chocolate Chip Oatmeal Cookies

These chocolate chip oatmeal cookies, developed by David Ogonowksi, a former pastry chef at Olives restaurant in Charlestown, MA, don't resemble the recipe for the chunky, earthy cookies found on the oat box packaging or the classic ones found on chocolate chip bags. Instead the flavor is more delicate and the texture more shortbread-like: once you try these you won't go back to either.

The difference between old-fashioned oats and quick oats is simply that the quick oats are cut into smaller pieces for faster cooking. Since you are crushing the oats even further, it makes no difference at all in this recipe.

1¼ cups (2½ sticks) unsalted butter,
   at room temperature

½ cup white sugar

1 cup light brown sugar

1 large egg, at room temperature

1 large egg yolk, at room temperature

1 tablespoon vanilla extract

1 cup quick-cooking or old-fashioned oats,
   pulsed well in a food processor

2 cups all-purpose white flour

1 teaspoon baking powder

1 teaspoon baking soda

1 teaspoon kosher salt

3 cups semi-sweet chocolate morsels or
   1 pound semi-sweet chocolate, chunked
   or roughly grated

Preheat the oven to 325°F. Line a cookie sheet with parchment paper.

Place the butter and sugars in the bowl of a mixer fitted with the paddle attachment and mix until smooth and creamy. Scrape down the sides of the bowl, add the egg, egg yolk and vanilla, one at a time, mixing well between additions. Scrape down the sides of the bowl, add the oats, flour, baking powder, baking soda and salt and mix until everything is well incorporated. Scrape down the sides of the bowl, add the chocolate and mix again.

Drop the dough by heaping teaspoons about 2 inches apart on the prepared cookie sheet. Alternatively, you can roll the dough into a log (see page 4). Transfer to the oven and bake until the cookies begin to brown at the edges, 12 to 15 minutes. Cool on the cookie sheet. Transfer to a wire rack and repeat with the remaining dough.

Banana Nut Cookies

YIELD: ABOUT 3 DOZEN COOKIES

Family friend, fourteen-year-old Charlotte Fitts-Sprague, pronounced these soft, almost biscuit-like cookies "the cookie version of banana bread." Chocolate and peanut free, these are a great option for very young children. Feel free to omit the nuts entirely or substitute raisins, dried cranberries, semi-sweet chocolate chips or coconut.

¾ cup (1½ sticks) unsalted butter, at room temperature

⅔ cup light brown sugar

1 large egg, at room temperature

1 very over-ripe banana, mashed

2 teaspoons vanilla extract

1½ cups all-purpose white flour

1 cup quick-cooking or old-fashioned oats

½ teaspoon kosher salt

¼ teaspoon baking soda

1 cup walnuts or pecans, lightly toasted (see page 10) and coarsely chopped

Place the butter and sugar in the bowl of a mixer fitted with the paddle attachment and mix until smooth and creamy. Scrape down the sides of the bowl, add the egg, mashed banana and vanilla, one at a time, mixing well between additions. Scrape down the sides of the bowl, add the flour, oats, salt and baking soda and mix until everything is well incorporated. Scrape down the sides of the bowl, add the walnuts or pecans and mix until they are well distributed.

Form the dough into 2 logs and refrigerate for at least 2 hours and up to 2 weeks (see page 4) or freeze up to 2 months.

Preheat the oven to 325°F. Line a cookie sheet with parchment paper.

Cut the dough logs into ¼-inch-thick slices and place the slices 2 inches apart on the prepared cookie sheet. Transfer to the oven and bake until the cookies begin to brown at the edges, 11 to 12 minutes. Partially cool on the cookie sheet and transfer to a wire rack. Repeat with the remaining dough. Eat when warm!

Toasting Nuts

Preheat the oven to 350°F. Place nuts on a baking sheet or in a shallow pan, transfer to the oven and bake until lightly colored and fragrant, about 10 minutes. Set aside to cool.

Sandra Fairbank's
Tiny Poppy Seed Cookies

YIELD: ABOUT 6 DOZEN COOKIES

It's no surprise that my friend Sandra Fairbank, a designer and architect, would make shortbread-like cookies that are not only utterly delicious but are noted for their endearing diminutive size and beauty. Sandra usually makes these with poppy seeds but has been known to substitute chocolate nibs, cardamom seed, chopped pistachios, or chopped candied ginger.

Although these tiny black seeds are said to be harvested for opium, poppy seeds are one of the most common staples in American kitchens. Some describe them as having a bitter or peppery taste and thus they are often mixed with lemon zest (my addition) to complement the flavor.

1 cup (½ pound/2 sticks) unsalted butter, each stick cut into 4 pieces, at room temperature	2¼ cups all-purpose white flour
¾ cup white sugar	½ teaspoon baking powder
1 large egg, at room temperature	¼ teaspoon kosher salt
1 teaspoon vanilla extract	¼ cup poppy seeds
	2 tablespoons fresh lemon zest (optional)

Place the butter and sugar in the bowl of a mixer fitted with the paddle attachment and mix until smooth and creamy. Scrape down the sides of the bowl, add the egg and vanilla, one at a time, mixing well between additions. Scrape down the sides of the bowl, add the flour, baking powder and salt and mix until everything is well incorporated. Scrape down the sides of the bowl, add the poppy seeds and lemon zest, if desired, and mix until they are well distributed.

Divide the dough into three small balls and place each ball into the center of a large resealable plastic bag. Place each bag on the counter and, using a rolling pin, roll the dough from the center toward the edges until it is ¼ inch thick. Refrigerate for at least 1 hour and up to 2 days. Alternatively, you can roll the dough into a 1-inch log (see page 4).

continued on next page

Preheat the oven to 400°F. Remove 1 sheet of dough from the refrigerator at a time.

Using a 1-inch round cookie cutter, punch out cookies and place 1 inch apart on an ungreased cookie sheet. Transfer to the oven and bake until the cookies are golden brown, 7 to 10 minutes. Cool on the cookie sheet. Transfer to a wire rack and repeat with the remaining dough.

Pecan Sandies

When I told people that I was writing a cookie book, I can't believe how many asked me if I had included a recipe for pecan sandies. It seems everyone wants to relive their childhood. The problem is, to get really close to a pecan sandie, I had to use shortening, which I can't stand. Herewith: my buttery version, sandy still.

¾ pound (3 sticks) unsalted butter, at room temperature

1 cup white sugar

2 large eggs, at room temperature

1 tablespoon vanilla extract

1 tablespoon water, at room temperature

4 cups all-purpose white flour

1½ teaspoons kosher salt

¼ teaspoon baking soda

2½ cups pecans, lightly toasted (see page 10), cooled and very coarsely chopped (not ground!!)

Preheat the oven to 325°F.

Place the butter and sugar in the bowl of a mixer fitted with the paddle attachment and mix until smooth and creamy. Scrape down the sides of the bowl, add the eggs, vanilla and water, one at a time, mixing well between additions. Scrape down the sides of the bowl, add the flour, salt and baking soda, and mix until combined. Scrape down the sides of the bowl, add the pecans and mix again.

Form the dough into 1-inch balls and using your hand or the bottom of a water glass, press down until flattened. Place on an ungreased cookie sheet. Transfer to the oven and bake until the cookies are just beginning to brown on the edges, 17 to 20 minutes. Transfer to a wire rack. Let the cookie sheet cool completely between batches and repeat with the remaining dough.

German Chocolate Cookies

YIELD: 3 TO 4 DOZEN COOKIES

When I was a child, I used to love German chocolate cake, the classic chocolate cake filled and topped with a gooey pecan and coconut concoction, and ordered it whenever and wherever it was offered. I was sure it would be easy to mimic those flavors in a cookie, but that turned out to be no simple task. After testing and testing, I came up with this cookie: crisp and light in texture but rich and chocolate-y in flavor. It certainly rivals the cakes I had growing up.

Although I am not a milk drinker, these beg for a tall glass of cold whole milk or for an even more decadent treat, coconut ice cream.

¾ cup (1½ sticks) unsalted butter,
  at room temperature

1 cup light brown sugar

1 large egg, at room temperature

1 tablespoon vanilla extract

1½ cups all-purpose white flour

½ cup unsweetened Dutch process cocoa
  (I like Droste or Scharffen Berger)

1 teaspoon baking soda

½ teaspoon kosher salt

2 cups sweetened coconut flakes

1 cup pecans, lightly toasted and cooled
  (see page 10), coarsely chopped

4 ounces German's sweet chocolate,
  coarsely chopped

Preheat the oven to 350°F. Line a cookie sheet with parchment paper.

Place the butter and sugar in the bowl of a mixer fitted with the paddle attachment and mix until smooth and creamy. Scrape down the sides of the bowl, add the egg and vanilla, one at a time, mixing well between additions. Scrape down the sides of the bowl, add the flour, cocoa, baking soda and salt and mix until everything is well incorporated. Scrape down the sides of the bowl, add the coconut, pecans and chocolate and mix again.

Drop the dough by heaping teaspoons about 2 inches apart on the prepared cookie sheet. Alternatively, you can roll the dough into a log (see page 4). Transfer to the oven and bake until the underside of the cookie begins to firm up, 10 to 12 minutes. Cool on the cookie sheet. Transfer to a wire rack and repeat with the remaining dough.

White Chocolate and Dried Cranberry Cookies

YIELD: 3 TO 4 DOZEN COOKIES

Although technically not considered chocolate by the US Food and Drug Administration because of its lack of chocolate liquor, white chocolate is treated as chocolate for baking. Like all chocolate it contains cocoa solids and cocoa butter, which allows it to remain solid at room temperature. While its texture is similar to milk and dark chocolates, the additional sugar and flavoring (usually vanilla) make it even sweeter, resulting in a product that is better as an ingredient, rather than eaten on its own. The trendy combination of white chocolate and dried cranberries will no doubt eventually be considered a classic one.

1¼ cups (2½ sticks) unsalted butter,
   at room temperature

½ cup white sugar

1 cup light brown sugar

1 large egg, at room temperature

1 large egg yolk, at room temperature

1 tablespoon vanilla extract

1 cup quick-cooking or old-fashioned oats,

pulsed well in a food processor

2 cups all-purpose white flour

1 teaspoon baking powder

1 teaspoon baking soda

1 teaspoon kosher salt

12 ounces white chocolate, coarsely chopped

1 cup dried cranberries

Preheat the oven to 325°F. Line a cookie sheet with parchment paper.

Place the butter and sugars in the bowl of a mixer fitted with the paddle attachment and mix until smooth and creamy. Scrape down the sides of the bowl, add the egg, egg yolk and vanilla, one at a time, mixing well between additions. Scrape down the sides of the bowl, add the oats, flour, baking powder, baking soda and salt and mix until everything is well incorporated. Scrape down the sides of the bowl, add the chocolate and cranberries and mix again.

Drop the dough by heaping teaspoons about 2 inches apart on the prepared cookie sheet. Alternatively, you can roll the dough into a log (see page 4). Transfer to the oven and bake until the cookies begin to brown at the edges, 12 to 15 minutes. Cool on the cookie sheet. Transfer to a wire rack and repeat with the remaining dough.

Toasted Cashew and Orange Cookies

YIELD: 3 TO 4 DOZEN COOKIES

It's not often that I design a cookie around a specific ingredient or brand but Boyajian Orange Oil (www.boyajianinc.com) just begs to be used by anyone who loves the flavor of fresh citrus. Cold pressed from orange rinds (220 oranges in a 5-ounce bottle), Boyajian orange oil is fresher and more intense than any orange flavoring I have ever had. The combination with the buttery cashew is pure transcendence.

1¼ cups (2½ sticks) unsalted butter, at room temperature

½ cup white sugar

1 cup light brown sugar

1 large egg, at room temperature

1 large egg yolk, at room temperature

1 tablespoon vanilla extract

1½ teaspoons Boyajian Orange Oil

1 cup quick-cooking or old-fashioned oats, pulsed well in a food processor

2 cups all-purpose white flour

1 teaspoon baking powder

1 teaspoon baking soda

1 teaspoon kosher salt

2 cups cashews, lightly toasted (see page 10), cooled and chopped

Preheat the oven to 325°F. Line a cookie sheet with parchment paper.

Place the butter and sugars in the bowl of a mixer fitted with the paddle attachment and mix until smooth and creamy. Scrape down the sides of the bowl, add the egg, egg yolk, vanilla and orange oil, one at a time, mixing well between additions. Scrape down the sides of the bowl, add the oats, flour, baking powder, baking soda and salt and mix until everything is well incorporated. Scrape down the sides of the bowl, add the cashews and mix again.

Drop the dough by heaping teaspoons about 2 inches apart on the prepared cookie sheet. Alternatively, you can roll the dough into a log (see page 4). Transfer to the oven and bake until the cookies begin to brown at the edges, 12 to 15 minutes. Cool on the cookie sheet. Transfer to a wire rack and repeat with the remaining dough.

Mary Granfield's
Chocolate Walnut Cookies

YIELD: ABOUT 4 DOZEN COOKIES

Containing unsweetened chocolate, semi-sweet chocolate and semi-sweet chocolate chips, these cookies are a chocoholics dream come true: my daughter Lauren says, "I would seriously kill someone for these cookies." When I first tested this recipe, my plan was to give a few to my kids and bring the rest to Mary, who claims she doesn't get to eat them often enough. Needless to say, they never made it to Mary's.

2 ounces unsweetened chocolate

6 ounces semi-sweet chocolate

2 tablespoons unsalted butter

2 teaspoons finely ground coffee beans

¾ cup white sugar

2 large eggs, at room temperature

½ teaspoon vanilla extract

¼ cup all-purpose white flour

¼ teaspoon baking powder

⅛ teaspoon kosher salt

2¼ cups walnut pieces, lightly toasted (see page 10) and cooled

1 cup (6 ounces) semi-sweet chocolate chips

Preheat the oven to 350°F. Line a cookie sheet with parchment paper.

Place the unsweetened and semi-sweet chocolates (not the chocolate chips) and butter in the top of a double boiler (or set a metal bowl over a saucepan of simmering water) and cook over low heat until melted. Set aside to cool.

Place the coffee, sugar and eggs in a mixing bowl and using a whisk or electric beater, whip until the mixture increases in volume and lightens in color, 4 to 5 minutes. Add the vanilla and cooled chocolate mixture and mix until well combined.

Add the flour, baking powder and salt and mix until just combined. Using a wooden spoon or spatula, stir in the walnut pieces and chocolate chips. The mixture will be very thick and heavy and you are sure to think you have done something wrong.

Drop the dough by heaping teaspoons about 2 inches apart on the prepared cookie sheet. Transfer to the oven and bake until just done, 8 to 10 minutes. Transfer to a wire rack to cool for at least 30 minutes. Repeat with the remaining dough.

Pecan Shorties

Melting in texture, not too sweet and fantastically nutty, these shortbread cookies are just the thing to have with tea in the afternoon.

½ cup (¼ pound/1 stick) unsalted butter,
  at room temperature

⅓ cup confectioners' sugar, plus additional
  for tossing

¼ teaspoon kosher salt

1 teaspoon vanilla extract

1 cup all-purpose white flour

⅓ cup finely ground toasted pecans
  (see page 10)

Preheat the oven to 350°F.

Place the butter and sugar in the bowl of a mixer fitted with the paddle attachment and mix until smooth and creamy. Add the salt and vanilla and mix until well combined. Add the flour and pecans and mix until just combined.

Form the dough into 1-inch balls and place about 1 inch apart on an ungreased cookie sheet. Transfer to the oven and bake until the bottoms are golden, 10 to 12 minutes. Cool on the cookie sheet. When they have cooled completely, toss with the additional confectioners' sugar. Repeat with the remaining dough.

Chai Shortbread

YIELD: ABOUT 3 DOZEN COOKIES

Chai, the Hindi word meaning tea, has become a regular listing on tea menus across America. Masala chai, the one most readily available in the United States, is made with a black tea base, often Assam, combined with cinnamon, star anise, ginger, cardamom, peppercorns, and cloves. When added to the shortbread dough, these spicy flavors are rendered subtle and almost impossible to identify: so far, no one has guessed the ingredients in this cookie.

1 cup (½ pound/2 sticks) unsalted butter, at room temperature

⅓ cup confectioners' sugar

⅓ cup white sugar

2¼ cups all-purpose white flour

2 tablespoons loose chai tea leaves

2 teaspoons vanilla extract

1 teaspoon kosher salt

Place the butter and sugars in the bowl of a mixer fitted with the paddle attachment or the bowl of a food processor fitted with the mixing blade and mix until creamy. Scrape down the sides of the bowl, add the flour, tea leaves, vanilla and salt and scrape again. Form into 1½-inch-diameter logs and cover with parchment paper. Place the logs in a resealable plastic bag and refrigerate for at least 1 hour and up to 2 days, or freeze for up to 2 months.

Preheat the oven to 325°F. Line a cookie sheet with parchment paper.

With the tip of a very sharp knife, cut ⅜-inch slices of the dough and place 1 inch apart on the prepared cookie sheet. Transfer to the oven and bake until the cookies are just beginning to brown on the edges, about 20 minutes. Transfer to a wire rack to cool. Let the cookie sheet cool completely between batches and repeat with the remaining dough.

Paige Retus's Fudge-Topped Toffee Cookies

YIELD: ABOUT 2 DOZEN COOKIES

Boston's legendary Paige Retus is that rare and brilliant chef who is equally comfortable making simple desserts for home and complicated, breathtaking restaurant fare. Paige's toffee cookie, buttery and rich, is taken to a whole new level with the contrasting bitter-sweet chocolate and toasty pecans.

1 cup (½ pound/2 sticks) unsalted butter,
    at room temperature
1 cup light brown sugar
2 large egg yolks, at room temperature
2 cups all-purpose white flour

1 teaspoon kosher salt
4 ounces semi- or bitter-sweet chocolate,
    melted
½ cup pecans, lightly toasted
    (see page 10), cooled and coarsely chopped

Preheat the oven to 350°F. Line a cookie sheet with parchment paper.

Place the butter and sugar in the bowl of a mixer fitted with the paddle attachment and mix until smooth and creamy. Add the egg yolks, one at a time, mixing well between additions. Add the flour and salt and mix until well combined.

Form the dough into a ball, roll out on a lightly floured board and cut with a 2-inch cookie cutter. Place the cookies 2 inches apart on the prepared sheet and transfer to the oven. Bake until golden at the edges and medium firm to the touch, 12 to 15 minutes. Do not remove from the sheet until completely cooled.

Using the back of a spoon, smooth the melted chocolate in a circular motion onto the cookie (almost to the edge) and while it is wet, sprinkle with the nuts. When the chocolate is completely cooled, transfer the cookies to a wire rack and repeat with the remaining dough.

24

Espresso Shortbread

The obvious beverage of choice for this dark, almost bitter-sweet shortbread is espresso, but milk or red wine, on opposite ends of the spectrum, are also flawless companions.

1 cup (½ pound/2 sticks) unsalted butter, at room temperature
⅓ cup confectioners' sugar
⅓ cup white sugar

2¼ cups all-purpose white flour
2½ tablespoons finely ground espresso beans
2 teaspoons vanilla extract
1 teaspoon kosher salt

Place the butter and sugars in the bowl of a mixer fitted with the paddle attachment or the bowl of a food processor fitted with the mixing blade and mix until smooth and creamy. Scrape down the sides of the bowl, add the flour, ground espresso beans, vanilla and salt, mix well and scrape again. Form the dough into 1½-inch-diameter logs and cover with parchment paper. Place the logs in a resealable plastic bag and refrigerate for at least 1 hour and up to 2 days, or freeze for up to 2 months.

Preheat the oven to 325°F. Line a cookie sheet with parchment paper.

With the tip of a very sharp knife, cut ¼- to ½-inch slices of the dough and place 2 inches apart on the prepared pan. Transfer to the oven and bake until the cookies are just beginning to brown on the edges, about 20 minutes. Transfer to a wire rack to cool. Let the cookie sheet cool completely between batches and repeat with the remaining dough.

Vanilla Bean Sugar Cookies

Instead of using vanilla extract in this recipe, I replaced it with a whole vanilla bean, resulting in the best sugar cookie I've ever tasted. The little flecks of vanilla make this crisp, delicate, "crumble in your mouth" cookie absolutely stunning and refined.

1 vanilla bean, slit down the middle lengthwise and coarsely chopped	1 large egg, at room temperature
1 cup white sugar, plus additional for sprinkling	1 large egg yolk, at room temperature
1 cup (½ pound/2 sticks) unsalted butter, at room temperature	2½ cups all-purpose white flour
	1 teaspoon baking powder
	½ teaspoon kosher salt

Place the vanilla bean and sugar in the bowl of a food processor fitted with the steel blade and process until the mixture turns a very pale brown and the vanilla bean is almost completely incorporated into the sugar, 3 to 5 minutes.

Transfer the mixture to the bowl of a mixer fitted with the paddle attachment, add the butter and mix until smooth and creamy. Scrape down the sides of the bowl, add the egg and egg yolk, one at a time, mixing well between additions. Scrape down the sides of the bowl, add the flour, baking powder and salt and mix until everything is well incorporated.

Scrape down the sides of the bowl and form the dough into 2 balls. Place each ball into the center of a large resealable plastic bag. Place each bag on the counter and, using a rolling pin, roll the dough from the center toward the edges until it is between ⅛ and ¼ inch thick. Refrigerate for at least 1 hour and up to 2 days. Alternatively, you can form the dough into a 1-inch log (see page 4).

Preheat the oven to 375°F. Remove 1 sheet of dough from the refrigerator at a time.

Using any shape cookie cutter, punch out cookies and place 2 inches apart on an ungreased cookie sheet. Transfer to the oven and bake until the cookies are just starting to turn golden brown on the edges, 8 to 10 minutes. Cool on the cookie sheet. Transfer to a wire rack and repeat with the remaining dough.

Chocolate Raisin Walnut Oatmeal Cookies

YIELD: 3 TO 4 DOZEN COOKIES

These are big, robust, wonderful cookies—jam packed with stuff; you can vary the stuff by substituting milk or white chocolate chips, any kind of dried fruit and any kind of nut because what makes these unique is that there is a little bit of everything in them. All the combos just seem to work. These giant cookies are almost like trail mix in a cookie— which make them particularly great for camping trips.

1 cup (½ pound/2 sticks) unsalted butter, at room temperature

½ cup white sugar

¾ cup light brown sugar

2 large eggs, at room temperature

1 tablespoon vanilla extract

1 cup quick-cooking or old-fashioned oats, pulsed well in a food processor

2 cups all-purpose white flour

1 teaspoon baking powder

1 teaspoon baking soda

1 teaspoon ground cinnamon

1 teaspoon kosher salt

2 cups dark raisins or dried cranberries

2 cups walnuts, lightly toasted (see page 10) and cooled

2 cups (12 ounces) semi-sweet chocolate chips or butterscotch chips

Preheat the oven to 325°F. Line a cookie sheet with parchment paper.

Place the butter and sugars in the bowl of a mixer fitted with the paddle attachment and mix until smooth and creamy. Scrape down the sides of the bowl, add the eggs, one at a time, and vanilla, mixing well between additions. Scrape down the sides of the bowl, add the oats, flour, baking powder, baking soda, cinnamon and salt and mix until everything is well incorporated. Scrape down the sides of the bowl, add the raisins, walnuts and chips and mix again.

Drop the dough by heaping tablespoons about 2 inches apart on the prepared cookie sheet. Alternatively, you can roll the dough into a log (see page 4). Transfer to the oven and bake until the cookies begin to brown at the edges and are still soft in the middle, about 12 minutes. Cool on the cookie sheet. Transfer to a wire rack and repeat with the remaining dough.

Spicy Cocoa Cookies

YIELD: 3 TO 4 DOZEN COOKIES

When I started this book, I queried all my friends on their favorite homemade cookies. Emily Friedan and Susan Orlean, both longtime friends, offered up a recipe for "a great spicy cocoa cookie" that they'd each been making for years. The irony is that each realized during the phone calls that I had, in fact, given them the recipe about 20 years ago. I had completely forgotten about this spicy, black, buttery gem.

If you don't push these down after putting them on the baking sheet, they will make tiny, slightly bitter-sweet, spicy brownies. The dough is very stiff and if you want, you can roll the pieces in sugar before placing on the baking sheet. Note that this recipe calls for using a raw egg white in the icing. Use only fresh eggs from a reliable source, or don't make the recipe if you feel uncertain.

FOR THE COOKIES:

1½ cups (¾ pound/3 sticks) unsalted butter, at room temperature

1¾ cups white sugar

2 large eggs, at room temperature

3 cups all-purpose white flour

1½ cups unsweetened cocoa powder

¼ teaspoon kosher salt

¼ teaspoon black pepper

¼ teaspoon cayenne pepper

½ teaspoon ground cinnamon

FOR THE ICING:

1 cup confectioners' sugar

1 large egg white

¼ teaspoon fresh lemon juice

Preheat the oven to 375°F. Line a cookie sheet with parchment paper.

Place the butter and sugar in the bowl of a mixer fitted with the paddle attachment and mix until smooth and creamy. Scrape down the sides of the bowl and add the eggs, one at a time, mixing well between additions. Scrape down the sides of the bowl, add the remaining ingredients and mix until everything is well incorporated. Scrape down the sides of the bowl and mix again.

Drop the dough by heaping teaspoons about 2 inches apart on the prepared cookie sheet. Using your hand or the bottom of a glass, press down until they are flattened. Alternatively, you can roll the dough into a log (see page 4).

continued on next page

Transfer to the oven and bake until the cookies begin to brown at the edges, 8 to 10 minutes. Cool on the cookie sheet. Transfer to a wire rack and repeat with the remaining dough.

While the cookies are cooling, make the icing: Place the sugar, egg white and lemon juice in a food processor fitted with the steel blade and process until smooth. Using the back of a spoon, smooth the icing in a circular motion onto the cooled cookies, almost to the edge.

Orange Almond Cookies

YIELD: ABOUT 3 DOZEN COOKIES

Steel ground yellow cornmeal, stone ground cornmeal, and white or yellow cornmeal (three types of flour made from ground maize, or dried corn) are all readily available in most American supermarkets. The main difference between each one is the amount of the corn kernel used, resulting in more or less texture and more or less nutritional value. I like the gritty texture of the steel ground (more texture, more value) but this is really a matter of personal taste. White and yellow cornmeal are most commonly used for baking. Take your pick.

¼ cup almonds, lightly toasted (see page 10), cooled and finely ground

½ cup (¼ pound/1 stick) unsalted butter, at room temperature

¼ cup plus 2 tablespoons white sugar

1 teaspoon freshly grated orange zest

1 large egg, at room temperature

2 tablespoons frozen orange juice concentrate, thawed

¾ cup all-purpose white flour

¼ cup cornmeal

¼ teaspoon kosher salt

Place the ground almonds, butter, sugar and orange zest in the bowl of a mixer fitted with the paddle attachment and mix until creamy. Scrape down the sides of the bowl, add the egg and orange juice concentrate, one at a time, mixing well between additions. Scrape down the sides of the bowl, add the remaining ingredients and mix until everything is well incorporated. Scrape down the sides of the bowl and mix again.

Form into 1½-inch-diameter logs and cover with parchment paper. Place the logs in a resealable plastic bag and refrigerate for at least 1 hour and up to 2 days, or freeze for up to 2 months.

Preheat the oven to 350°F. Line a cookie sheet with parchment paper.

With the tip of a very sharp knife, cut ¼ to ⅜-inch slices of the dough and place 2 inches apart on the prepared pan. Transfer to the oven and bake until the cookies are just beginning to brown on the edges, 12 to 14 minutes. Transfer the cookies to a wire rack to cool. Let the cookie sheet cool completely between batches and repeat with the remaining dough.

Jenny deBell's Snickerdoodles

YIELD: 3 TO 4 DOZEN COOKIES

My son Ben's current favorite, it's hard not to like a cookie with a name like this, if even just to say it out loud. Some say its roots are from New England, while others claim Pennsylvania Dutch. Still others say Germany, claiming it comes from the word *schneckennudeln*, meaning "crinkly noodles," which makes no sense to me. Whatever its origin, this classic sugar cookie is all about the cinnamon sugar!

FOR THE COOKIES:

1 cup (½ pound/2 sticks) unsalted butter, margarine or shortening or a combination, at room temperature

1½ cups white sugar

2 large eggs, at room temperature

2¾ cups all-purpose white flour

2 teaspoons cream of tartar

1 teaspoon baking soda

½ teaspoon kosher salt

FOR THE CINNAMON SUGAR:

2 tablespoons sugar

1 tablespoon ground cinnamon

Line a cookie sheet with parchment paper.

To make the cookies: Place the butter and sugar in the bowl of a mixer fitted with the paddle attachment and mix until smooth and creamy. Scrape down the sides of the bowl, add the eggs, one at a time, mixing well between additions. Scrape down the sides of the bowl, add the remaining ingredients and mix until everything is well incorporated. Scrape down the sides of the bowl and mix again. Cover and refrigerate for at least 2 hours and up to overnight.

To make the cinnamon sugar: Place the sugar and cinnamon on a plate and mix until well combined.

To form the cookies: break off small pieces and roll into 1-inch balls. Roll the balls in the cinnamon sugar and place 2 inches apart on the prepared cookie sheet. Using your hand or the bottom of a water glass, press down until flattened.

Preheat the oven to 400°F. Transfer to the oven and bake until the cookies begin to brown at the edges, 8 to 10 minutes. Cool on the cookie sheet. Transfer to a wire rack and repeat with the remaining dough.

Brown Sugar Cookies

YIELD: ABOUT 4 DOZEN COOKIES

Crispy on the edges and soft in the middle, these cookies are quintessential childhood fare. The brown sugar gives them a fuller flavor than white and adds a richer taste to the cookies. If you don't have any on hand (and are feeling ambitious) simply substitute 1¼ cups white sugar and 4 teaspoons molasses.

¾ cup (1½ sticks) unsalted butter, at room temperature

1¼ cups dark brown sugar

1 large egg, at room temperature

2 cups all-purpose white flour

2 teaspoons baking soda

½ teaspoon ground ginger

½ teaspoon ground cinnamon

½ teaspoon kosher salt

Preheat the oven to 375°F.

Place the butter and sugar in the bowl of a mixer fitted with the paddle attachment and mix until smooth and creamy. Scrape down the sides of the bowl, add the egg and mix well. Scrape down the sides of the bowl, add the remaining ingredients and mix until everything is well incorporated. Scrape down the sides of the bowl and mix again.

Drop large teaspoons of dough onto an ungreased cookie sheet about 2 inches apart and bake until the edges are just brown, 8 to 12 minutes. For crispy cookies, let cool on the sheet. Let the cookie sheet cool completely between batches and repeat with the remaining dough.

Pogasca

E dith Orlean is not one to part with her favorite recipes so I was truly honored when she offered me this traditional Hungarian *pogasca*. Fluffy, buttery and crisp, they are somewhat of a cross between a biscuit and a butter cookie. Cited in Hungarian folktales as the perfect food for journeys, this is exactly what Edith prepared for her family's trips when her children were young.

3 cups all-purpose white flour

¼ cup white sugar

2 teaspoons baking powder

¼ teaspoon kosher salt

¾ pound (3 sticks) unsalted butter,
    frozen and grated

1 cup sour cream

3 large egg yolks, at room temperature

1 large egg white, beaten with a fork

Preheat the oven to 400°F. Line a baking sheet with parchment paper.

Place the flour, sugar, baking powder and salt in the bowl of a mixer fitted with the paddle attachment and mix until the ingredients are well incorporated. While the mixer is going, add the frozen butter, sour cream and egg yolks, one at a time, mixing well between additions, until it forms a smooth dough.

Roll the dough out to ½-inch thickness, punch out cookies with 1-inch cookie cutters and transfer to the prepared cookie sheet and place about 2 inches apart. Using a sharp knife, make a crisscross pattern on top. Brush with the egg white and transfer to the oven. Bake for 5 minutes and then reduce the oven to 350°F. Bake until golden brown, about 20 minutes. Transfer to a wire cooling rack and repeat with the remaining dough.

Cream Cheese Cookies

S tarting with a classic butter cookie and replacing some of the butter with cream cheese and using an egg yolk instead of a whole egg makes these cookies very rich, very dense and very creamy.

1 cup (½ pound/2 sticks) unsalted butter,
  at room temperature

4 ounces cream cheese, at room temperature

1 cup white sugar

1 large egg yolk, at room temperature

1 teaspoon vanilla extract

2½ cups all-purpose white flour

¾ teaspoon kosher salt

Preheat the oven to 325°F.

Place the butter, cream cheese and sugar in the bowl of a mixer fitted with the paddle attachment and mix until smooth and creamy. Scrape down the sides of the bowl, add the egg yolk and vanilla, mixing well between additions. Scrape down the sides of the bowl, add the remaining ingredients and mix until everything is well incorporated. Scrape down the sides of the bowl and mix again.

Drop large teaspoons of dough onto an ungreased cookie sheet about 2 inches apart and bake until the edges are just brown, 14 to 16 minutes. Let cool on the sheet. Transfer to a wire rack and repeat with the remaining dough.

Date Nut Cookies

YIELD: 3 TO 4 DOZEN COOKIES

Eating this cookie version of date nut bread, chock full of dates and walnuts, will make you feel just a little virtuous. These are great served as part of a brunch with bagels and cream cheese.

1 cup (½ pound/2 sticks) unsalted butter, at room temperature	2 cups all-purpose white flour
½ cup white sugar	1 teaspoon baking powder
¾ cup light brown sugar	1 teaspoon baking soda
2 large eggs, at room temperature	1 teaspoon ground cinnamon
1 tablespoon vanilla extract	1 teaspoon kosher salt
1 cup quick-cooking or old-fashioned oats, pulsed well in a food processor	3 cups dates, coarsely chopped
	3 cups walnuts, lightly toasted and cooled (see page 10)

Preheat the oven to 325°F. Line a cookie sheet with parchment paper.

Place the butter and sugars in the bowl of a mixer fitted with the paddle attachment and blend until creamy. Add the eggs, one at a time, and the vanilla, mixing well between additions. Scrape down the sides of the bowl, add the remaining ingredients, except the dates and walnuts, and mix until everything is well incorporated. Scrape down the sides of the bowl, add the dates and walnuts and mix again.

Drop the dough by heaping teaspoons about 2 inches apart on the prepared cookie sheet. Alternatively, you can roll the dough into a log (see page 4). Transfer to the oven and bake until the cookies begin to brown at the edges and are still soft in the middle, about 12 minutes. Cool on the cookie sheet. Transfer to a wire rack and repeat with the remaining dough.

Jeff Conti's
Peanut Butter "Cookies"

YIELD: ABOUT 30 COOKIES

B e sure to read this recipe thoroughly before beginning. When Jeff sent me this recipe, I was sure he had left out the flour since there wasn't any in the list of ingredients. These were cookies, after all. But indeed, there is no flour, which makes these cookies, made mostly of peanuts and peanut butter, the best, most peanut-y peanut butter cookies I have had.

2 tablespoons unsalted butter,
   at room temperature

1 cup creamy or chunky peanut butter,
   at room temperature

1 cup white sugar

1 large egg, at room temperature

1 teaspoon baking soda

½ teaspoon kosher salt

¾ cup roasted peanuts, coarsely chopped
   (optional)

Preheat the oven to 350°F. Line a cookie sheet with parchment paper.

Place the butter, peanut butter and sugar in the bowl of a mixer fitted with the paddle attachment and mix until smooth and creamy. Scrape down the sides of the bowl, add the egg and mix until well incorporated. Scrape down the sides of the bowl, add the baking soda, salt and peanuts, if desired, and mix again. The dough will be really crumbly and not seem to come together well: *not to worry*.

Form the dough into 1½-inch balls and place 2 inches apart on the prepared cookie sheet. Using your hand or the bottom of a water glass, press down until flattened, and then, using a sharp knife, make a crisscross pattern on top. Transfer to the oven and bake until the cookies are just beginning to brown, about 10 minutes. Remove the cookies from the cookie sheet and transfer to a wire rack to cool. Let the cookie sheet cool completely between batches and repeat with the remaining dough.

Savory Cheese Cookies

Ellen Sturgis grew up making these savory "cookies" and continues to make them with her daughter Rozzie every Christmas. Come December, there is always a full tin in her kitchen; when she runs out, she just whips up another batch to bring to friends for the holidays. They last forever (well, a month) if they don't get eaten immediately. But honestly, it's hard to eat just one.

1 cup (½ pound/2 sticks) butter, at room temperature

½ pound sharp cheddar cheese, grated
2½ to 3 cups all-purpose white flour

Preheat the oven to 350°F.

Place the butter in the bowl of a mixer fitted with the paddle attachment and mix until smooth and creamy. Scrape down the sides of the bowl, add the cheese and mix until everything is well incorporated. Scrape down the sides of the bowl, gradually add the flour and mix again until the dough looks dry. The dough shouldn't feel sticky.

Roll into walnut size balls, place 2 inches apart on an ungreased cookie sheet and press the balls down with the tines of a fork. Transfer to the oven and bake until the bottoms begin to brown, 15 to 18 minutes. Transfer to a wire rack to cool. Let the cookie sheet cool completely between batches and repeat with the remaining dough.

cookies

Cornmeal Shortbread and Jam Tots

These unusual cookies are a variation on the classic jam tot, a sugar cookie with a jam-filled indentation. Here I have replaced some of the flour with cornmeal, resulting in a lovely grainy texture. You don't have to make a jam-filled indentation but it adds a contrasting sweetness to the rustic cornmeal, like the classic corn muffin filled with jam.

½ cup (¼ pound/1 stick) unsalted butter, at room temperature

⅔ cup white sugar, plus additional for rolling (optional)

1 large egg, at room temperature

1 large egg yolk, at room temperature

1¼ cups all-purpose white flour

1 cup yellow cornmeal

Grated zest of 1 orange (optional)

1½ teaspoons baking powder

½ teaspoon kosher salt

Strawberry or raspberry jam

Preheat the oven to 325°F.

Place the butter and sugar in the bowl of a mixer fitted with the paddle attachment and mix until smooth and creamy. Scrape down the sides of the bowl, add the egg and egg yolk, one at a time, mixing well between additions. Scrape down the sides of the bowl, add the remaining ingredients, except the jam, and mix until everything is well incorporated. Scrape down the sides of the bowl and mix again.

Divide the dough into 30 balls and, if desired, roll in sugar. Place the balls 2 inches apart on an ungreased cookie sheet. Using your finger or the back of a measuring teaspoon, make an indentation in the middle of each ball. Transfer to the oven and bake until they begin to brown on the bottom, about 18 minutes.

Remove the cookies to a wire rack and when they have cooled completely, fill the indentation with jam. Let the cookie sheet cool completely between batches and repeat with the remaining dough.

Irish Lace Cookies

YIELD: ABOUT 2 DOZEN COOKIES

Not your basic oatmeal cookie, these flat, delicate, lacy cookies get their name from Irish lace. Refined, lovely with tea, elegant and grown up, these are great served atop ice cream. If you're looking for something more ornamental, wrap them around a cylinder right when they come out of the oven, so that they form a sort of curved half moon.

½ cup (¼ pound/1 stick) unsalted butter, at room temperature

¾ cup light brown sugar

2 tablespoons water

1 teaspoon vanilla extract

¼ cup all-purpose white flour

1¼ cups quick-cooking or old-fashioned oats

Preheat the oven to 350°F. Line a cookie sheet with parchment paper.

Place the butter and sugar in the bowl of a mixer fitted with the paddle attachment and mix until smooth and creamy. Scrape down the sides of the bowl, add the water and vanilla and mix well. Scrape down the sides of the bowl, add the remaining ingredients and mix until everything is well incorporated. Scrape down the sides of the bowl and mix again.

Divide the dough into 24 portions and drop about 2 inches apart on the prepared cookie sheet. Transfer to the oven and bake until the cookies begin to brown at the edges and are still soft in the middle, 10 to 12 minutes. Be sure to immediately move the cookies around on the cookie sheet as soon as they come out of the oven or they will stick. Cool on the cookie sheet. Transfer to a wire rack and repeat with the remaining dough.

Chewy Molasses Cookies

YIELD: 3 TO 4 DOZEN COOKIES

Although I am a huge fan of crunchy, flat cookies, I wanted to include a recipe for a moister, chewy version of a molasses cookie. This cookie competes in a big way with Ben's Molasses Cookies (see page 5), my son's all-time favorite, and now I can't decide which one I like best (so, of course, I just make both).

1½ cups (¾ pound/3 sticks) unsalted butter, at room temperature	4 cups all-purpose white flour
2 cups white sugar	1 tablespoon baking soda
2 large eggs, at room temperature	2 teaspoons ground cinnamon
½ cup molasses	1 teaspoon ground nutmeg
	1 teaspoon kosher salt

Preheat the oven to 375°F. Line a cookie sheet with parchment paper.

Place the butter and sugar in the bowl of a mixer fitted with the paddle attachment and mix until smooth and creamy. Scrape down the sides of the bowl, add the eggs, one at a time, and the molasses, mixing well between additions. Scrape down the sides of the bowl, add the remaining ingredients and mix until everything is well incorporated. Scrape down the sides of the bowl and mix again.

Drop the dough by heaping teaspoons about 2 inches apart on the prepared cookie sheet. Alternatively, you can roll the dough into a log (see page 4).

Transfer to the oven and bake until the cookies begin to brown at the edges and are still soft in the middle, about 12 minutes. Cool on the cookie sheet. Transfer to a wire rack and repeat with the remaining dough.

Olive Oil and Wine Cookies

YIELD: 32 COOKIES

These are definitely among the strangest cookies in this book but I find them irresistible: hard and almost cracker-like, while the flavors of the olive oil and the wine are understated you can identify them if you pay close attention. Great with cheese and red wine either as an hors d'oeuvre or after dinner. I like to flatten them but it's not necessary.

This is not a dough to let sit: make the dough and then bake the cookies right away.

2 cups all-purpose white flour

1 cup white sugar

½ teaspoon baking soda

½ teaspoon kosher salt

¼ teaspoon freshly ground black pepper

½ cup extra virgin olive oil

¼ cup dry red wine

Preheat the oven to 350°F. Line a cookie sheet with parchment paper.

Place the flour, sugar, baking soda, salt and pepper in the bowl of a mixer fitted with the paddle attachment and mix until everything is incorporated. Gradually, while the paddle is moving, add the olive oil and wine. Scrape down the sides of the bowl and mix again.

Drop the dough by tablespoons about 2 inches apart on the prepared cookie sheet. The dough tends to separate so bake these right away. If you like flatter cookies, using your hand or the bottom of a water glass, press down until flattened.

Transfer to the oven and bake until the cookies are lightly browned, 12 to 15 minutes. Cool on the cookie sheet. Transfer to a wire rack and repeat with the remaining dough.

Annie Fischel's Meringues

When I met Linette Liebling we discovered that we had three good friends in common. The more we got to know each other, it seemed there was barely a soul I knew who Linette didn't also know, no matter how remote. When Linette sent me this recipe, I asked her who Annie was. When she told me, I realized I had gone to high school in New York with her. Of course.

2 large egg whites, at room temperature

1 teaspoon vanilla extract

¾ cup white sugar

⅛ teaspoon kosher salt

⅛ teaspoon cream of tartar

1 cup (6 ounces) semi-sweet chocolate chips

¼ cup lightly toasted (see page 10) and cooled, chopped walnuts (optional)

Preheat the oven to 300°F. Line a cookie sheet with parchment paper.

Place the egg whites in a large mixing bowl and beat until soft peaks form. Gradually add the vanilla, sugar, salt and cream of tartar. Using a wooden spoon, gently mix in the chocolate chips and walnuts.

Drop by rounded spoonfuls onto the prepared sheet and transfer to the oven. Bake until firm and dry, about 25 minutes. Transfer to a wire rack. Let the cookie sheet cool completely between batches and repeat with the remaining dough.

Celina Windzio's Nantucket Peanut Butter Cookies

YIELD: ABOUT 3 DOZEN COOKIES

For many years, Celina was my friend Sharon Smith's mother's helper. In Celina's native country of Germany they don't make peanut butter cookies—or at least she had never tried them—nor had she had chocolate chip cookies. She adapted this from a recipe she found in the Nantucket *Inquirer and Mirror*, a local paper, and made them for Sharon's three daughters, Alexandra, Julia and Hilary, summer after summer.

½ cup (¼ pound/1 stick) unsalted butter, at room temperature

½ cup peanut butter

½ cup white sugar, plus additional for rolling

½ cup light brown sugar

1 large egg, at room temperature

1 teaspoon vanilla extract

1½ cups all-purpose white flour

¾ teaspoon baking soda

¼ teaspoon kosher salt

Semi-sweet chocolate chips (optional, but strongly recommended)

Preheat the oven to 375°F. Line a cookie sheet with parchment paper.

Place the butter, peanut butter and sugars in the bowl of a mixer fitted with the paddle attachment and mix until smooth and creamy. Scrape down the sides of the bowl, add the egg and vanilla, mixing well between additions. Scrape down the sides of the bowl, add the remaining ingredients and mix until everything is well incorporated. Scrape down the sides of the bowl and mix again.

To form the cookies: break off small pieces and roll into 1-inch balls. Roll the balls in the sugar and place 2 inches apart on the prepared cookie sheet. Using the tines of a fork, push down gently until you have made a crisscross pattern on top. Be careful not to press too hard, as they get flat while baking. Transfer to the oven and bake until the cookies begin to brown at the edges, about 10 to 12 minutes. Cool on the cookie sheet for 2 to 3 minutes and then transfer to a wire rack. Let the cookie sheet cool completely between batches and repeat with the remaining dough.

Nancy Olin's
Chocolate Chip Cookies

YIELD: ABOUT 3 DOZEN COOKIES

Many years ago, I hosted a party where all I did was supply champagne and milk. An odd combination perhaps but the party had a theme: a chocolate chip cookie bake-off. I have, at times, made my living by cooking and yet, my chocolate chip cookies have not always been stellar. The party was a great success: I did almost no work, and my friends got to eat an obscene amount of cookies. Nancy's recipe was the hands-down winner. (And in case you were wondering: my chocolate chip cookies are now excellent.)

Nancy likes these best warm out of the oven or frozen, eaten directly from the freezer.

1 cup (½ pound/2 sticks) unsalted butter, at room temperature, almost runny

1 cup light brown sugar

¾ cup white sugar

2 large eggs, at room temperature

1 generous teaspoon vanilla extract

2 cups all-purpose white flour

¾ teaspoon baking soda

1 teaspoon kosher salt

2 cups semi-sweet chocolate chips

Preheat the oven to 340°F. (You don't have to measure this, just set your thermometer between 325° and 350°F.) Line a cookie sheet with parchment paper.

Place the butter and sugars in the bowl of a mixer fitted with the paddle attachment and mix until smooth and creamy. Scrape down the sides of the bowl, add the eggs and vanilla, mixing well between additions. Scrape down the sides of the bowl, add the flour, baking soda and salt and mix until everything is well incorporated. Scrape down the sides of the bowl, add the chocolate chips and mix again.

Drop the cookies by heaping tablespoons 2 inches apart onto the prepared pan. Transfer to the oven and bake until the cookies begin to brown on the edges but are soft in middle, 10 to 12 minutes. Cool on the cookie sheet for 2 to 3 minutes and then transfer to a wire rack. Let the cookie sheet cool completely between batches and repeat with the remaining dough.

Sharon Smith's Spice Cookies

YIELD: ABOUT 30 COOKIES

Reminiscent of the flavor of gingerbread and similar in texture to both molasses cookies and gingersnaps, these cookies are not for the fainthearted: they are spicy and intense.

¼ cup (½ stick) unsalted butter,
  at room temperature

1 cup (packed) dark brown sugar

½ cup vegetable shortening

1 large egg, at room temperature

¼ cup mild (light) molasses

2 cups all-purpose white flour

¾ cup finely chopped crystallized ginger

2½ teaspoons ground ginger

2 teaspoons baking soda

1 teaspoon ground cinnamon

1 teaspoon ground cloves

¾ teaspoon kosher salt

Place the butter, sugar and shortening in the bowl of a mixer fitted with the paddle attachment and mix until smooth and creamy. Scrape down the sides of the bowl, add the egg and molasses, mixing well between additions. Scrape down the sides of the bowl, add the remaining ingredients and mix until everything is well incorporated. Scrape down the sides of the bowl and mix again. Cover and refrigerate at least 1 hour and up to 2 days.

Preheat the oven to 350°F. Line a cookie sheet with parchment paper.

To form the cookies: break off small pieces and roll into 1-inch balls. Roll the balls in the sugar and place 2 inches apart on the prepared cookie sheet. Transfer to the oven and bake until they are cracked on top but still soft to the touch, about 12 minutes. Cool on the cookie sheet. Transfer to a wire rack and repeat with the remaining dough.

Crispy Chocolate Chip Cookies

YIELD: ABOUT 3 DOZEN COOKIES

I haven't yet had a taster who could ascertain the ingredients in these cookies. The crispy rice cereal adds crunch, which makes these great for anyone who has nut allergies but misses the texture that nuts offer.

½ cup (¼ pound/1 stick) unsalted butter, at room temperature

¼ cup white sugar

¼ cup light brown sugar

1 large egg, at room temperature

1 cup all-purpose white flour

½ teaspoon baking powder

½ teaspoon kosher salt

1 cup (6 ounces) semi-sweet chocolate chips

1 cup crispy rice cereal

Preheat the oven to 375°F. Line a cookie sheet with parchment paper.

Place the butter and sugars in the bowl of a mixer fitted with the paddle attachment and mix until smooth and creamy. Scrape down the sides of the bowl, add the egg and mix well. Scrape down the sides of the bowl, add the remaining ingredients, except the chocolate chips and crispy rice cereal, and mix until everything is well incorporated. Scrape down the sides of the bowl, add the chocolate chips and crispy rice cereal and mix again.

Drop the dough by heaping teaspoons about 2 inches apart on the prepared cookie sheet. Alternatively, you can roll the dough into a log (see page 4). Transfer to the oven and bake until the cookies begin to brown at the edges, 8 to 10 minutes. Cool on the cookie sheet. Transfer to a wire rack and repeat with the remaining dough.

Cocoa Toffee Chunk Cookies

When my kids return from Halloween trick-or-treating they dump their haul out on the dining room floor and classify it by size, flavor and sometimes by desirability. After the first few days they completely forget about the candy but before I toss it out, I excavate their bags for yummy things to put into cookies. This combination, basically a cocoa cookie with almonds and Heath bar, is one of the best so far: now I search their bags for Heath bars.

1 cup (½ pound/2 sticks) unsalted butter, at room temperature

1 cup white sugar

2 large eggs, at room temperature

2 cups all-purpose white flour

1 cup unsweetened cocoa powder

1 teaspoon baking soda

½ teaspoon baking powder

½ teaspoon kosher salt

2 cups coarsely chopped Heath bars (about 12 ounces, crushed Heath bars are also available in most grocery stores)

½ cup coarsely chopped or sliced toasted almonds (see page 10)

Preheat the oven to 350°F. Line a cookie sheet with parchment paper.

Place the butter and sugar in the bowl of a mixer fitted with the paddle attachment and mix until smooth and creamy. Scrape down the sides of the bowl, add the eggs, one at a time, mixing well between additions. Scrape down the sides of the bowl, add the flour, cocoa powder, baking soda, baking powder and salt and mix until everything is well incorporated. Scrape down the sides of the bowl, add the chopped Heath bars and almonds, and mix again.

Drop the dough by heaping teaspoons about 2 inches apart on the prepared cookie sheet. Alternatively, you can roll the dough into a log (see page 4). Transfer to the oven and bake until the cookies begin to brown at the edges, 12 to 15 minutes. Cool on the cookie sheet. Transfer to a wire rack and repeat with the remaining dough.

Black Chocolate Oatmeal Cookies

Basically an oatmeal cookie in disguise, this chocolate-y oatmeal cookie is a winner for grown-ups who love chocolate but don't want too much sweetness. The bitterness of the cocoa powder results in a cookie that is slightly less sweet and slightly drier than its inspiration.

1 cup (½ pound/2 sticks) unsalted butter, at room temperature

1 cup dark brown sugar

½ cup white sugar

2 large eggs, at room temperature

2 tablespoons water

2½ cups quick-cooking or old-fashioned oats

1½ cups all-purpose white flour

½ cup unsweetened cocoa powder

½ teaspoon baking soda

½ teaspoon kosher salt

2 cups (12 ounces) semi-sweet chocolate chips

Preheat the oven to 375°F. Line a cookie sheet with parchment paper.

Place the butter and sugars in the bowl of a mixer fitted with the paddle attachment and mix until smooth and creamy. Scrape down the sides of the bowl, add the eggs, one at a time, and the water, mixing well between additions. Scrape down the sides of the bowl, add the remaining ingredients, except the chocolate chips, and mix until everything is well incorporated. Scrape down the sides of the bowl, add the chocolate chips, and mix again.

Drop the dough by heaping teaspoons about 2 inches apart on the prepared cookie sheet. Alternatively, you can roll the dough into a log (see page 4). Transfer to the oven and bake until the cookies begin to brown at the edges, 10 to 12 minutes. Cool on the cookie sheet. Transfer to a wire rack and repeat with the remaining dough.

Citrus Shortbread

I like to roll this lovely citrus shortbread into a log and slice it but you can also roll it out and cut it with cookie cutters: stars and hearts make these a welcome addition on a cookie plate. For Christmas I often wrap them in cellophane bags tied with ribbon. These are equally fitting in the summertime with fresh strawberries.

⅔ cup confectioners' sugar

⅔ cup white sugar

Grated zest of 6 well-washed lemons
   or 4 lemons and 3 limes

1 pound (4 sticks) unsalted butter,
   at room temperature

1 tablespoon plus 1 teaspoon vanilla extract

2 teaspoons kosher salt

4½ cups all-purpose white flour

Place the sugars and zest in the bowl of a mixer fitted with the paddle attachment and mix until well combined and almost gritty. Add the butter and mix until smooth and creamy. Scrape down the sides of the bowl, add the vanilla, and mix well. Scrape down the sides of the bowl, add the remaining ingredients and mix until everything is well incorporated. Scrape down the sides of the bowl and mix again.

Form into two 1½ -inch-diameter logs and cover with parchment paper. Place the logs in a resealable plastic bag and refrigerate at least 1 hour and up to 2 days, or freeze up to 2 months.

Preheat the oven to 325°F. Line a cookie sheet with parchment paper.

With the tip of a very sharp knife, cut ⅜-inch slices of the dough and place 2 inches apart on the prepared pan. Transfer to the oven and bake until the cookies are just beginning to brown on the edges, about 20 minutes. Transfer to a wire rack to cool. Let the cookie sheet cool completely between batches and repeat with the remaining dough.

Mexican Wedding Cookies

YIELD: ABOUT 5 DOZEN COOKIES

Nutty, crumbly, airy and yet dense, these melt-in-your-mouth cookies are almost impossible to stop eating. They can most easily be distinguished by the obligatory coating of confectioners' sugar on top; if you don't pop these tiny cookies directly in your mouth you will surely have lips and shirt full of powdered sugar.

1 cup (½ pound/2 sticks) unsalted butter,
at room temperature

¼ cup confectioners' sugar, plus additional
for rolling

1 teaspoon vanilla extract

2 cups all-purpose white flour

2 cups walnut halves, lightly toasted (see
page 10), cooled and finely ground

Preheat the oven to 375°F.

Place the butter and sugar in the bowl of a mixer fitted with the paddle attachment and mix until smooth and creamy. Scrape down the sides of the bowl, add the vanilla and mix again. Scrape down the sides of the bowl, add the remaining ingredients and mix until everything is well incorporated. Scrape down the sides of the bowl and mix again.

Form the dough into 1-inch balls and place 2 inches apart on an ungreased cookie sheet. Transfer to the oven and bake until the cookies are just beginning to brown on the edges, about 15 minutes. Transfer the cookies to a wire rack, cool and then roll in confectioners' sugar. Let the cookie sheet cool completely between batches and repeat with the remaining dough.

Agnes Wazenski's Applesauce Butterscotch Cookies

YIELD: ABOUT 3 DOZEN COOKIES

My walking partner Ann Marchetti claims to be a cookie fiend but in truth her favorite cookie is the low-fat, low-sugar one her mother, Agnes, created (which in my mind, does not make her a true cookie fiend). Although the combination seems odd, I decided to trust Ann and not only were these tasty, they were the most popular cookie, among many, at a recent party.

Ann says you can substitute nuts or dried fruit for the butterscotch chips.

½ cup (¼ pound/1 stick) unsalted butter or margarine, at room temperature

1 cup light brown sugar or Splenda

½ cup white sugar or Splenda

1½ cups applesauce

2 large eggs, at room temperature

1 teaspoon vanilla extract

1½ cups all-purpose white flour

1 teaspoon baking powder

1 teaspoon baking soda

1 teaspoon cinnamon

¼ teaspoon ground clove

¼ teaspoon kosher salt

3 cups quick-cooking oats

3 cups (18 ounces) butterscotch chips

Preheat the oven to 350°F. Line a cookie with parchment paper.

Place the butter and sugars in the bowl of a mixer fitted with the paddle attachment and mix until smooth and creamy. Scrape down the sides of the bowl, add the applesauce, eggs, one at a time, and vanilla, mixing well between additions. Scrape down the sides of the bowl, add the flour, baking powder, baking soda, spices and salt and mix until everything is well incorporated. Scrape down the sides of the bowl, add the oatmeal and chips and mix again.

Place heaping teaspoonfuls of dough 2 inches apart on the prepared cookie sheet and transfer to the oven. Bake until the edges begin to firm up, about 15 minutes. Transfer to a wire rack to cool. Let the cookie sheet cool completely between batches and repeat with the remaining dough.

Almond Butter Oat Cookies

An earthy alternative to peanut butter cookies, with a more subtle flavor, these cookies are good for those who have peanut butter allergies but can eat tree nuts.

   The rare cookie that tastes best after it has cooled, if you can stand to wait that long, it's well worth it. Chopped almonds and chocolate chips are good optional additions.

1 cup (½ pound/2 sticks) unsalted butter,
   at room temperature
½ cup white sugar
1 cup light brown sugar
1 cup almond, peanut or cashew butter
2 large eggs, at room temperature

1 tablespoon vanilla extract
1½ cups old-fashioned oats, ground,
   if desired
2 cups all-purpose white flour
2 teaspoons baking soda
1 teaspoon kosher salt

Preheat the oven to 350°F. Line a cookie sheet with parchment paper.

Place the butter and sugars in the bowl of a mixer fitted with the paddle attachment and mix until smooth and creamy. Scrape down the sides of the bowl, add the nut butter and the eggs, one at a time, and vanilla, mixing well between additions. Scrape down the sides of the bowl, add the remaining ingredients and mix until everything is well incorporated. Scrape down the sides of the bowl and mix again.

Place heaping teaspoonfuls 2 inches apart on the prepared cookie sheet and transfer to the oven. Alternatively, form into four 1½-inch-diameter logs (see page 4). Bake until the edges begin to firm up, about 15 minutes. For crispy cookies, let cool on the cookie sheet. Transfer to a wire rack and repeat with the remaining dough.

Almond Crescents

Similar to Mexican Wedding Cookies (see page 62) but traditionally shaped into crescents, these are not as nutty, but are more like a nutty butter cookie.

Almonds are lower in carbohydrates and saturated fat and higher in calcium than any other tree nuts. Full of vitamin E, magnesium, protein and potassium, almonds are packed with antioxidants, which promote a healthy heart.

1 cup (½ pound/2 sticks) unsalted butter, at room temperature

¾ cup confectioners' sugar, plus additional for rolling

1 tablespoon whole milk

1 teaspoon vanilla extract

2¼ cups all-purpose white flour

½ cup almonds, lightly toasted (see page 10), cooled, and finely ground

Pinch of kosher salt

Place the butter and sugar in the bowl of a mixer fitted with the paddle attachment and mix until smooth and creamy. Scrape down the sides of the bowl, add the milk and vanilla, mixing well between additions. Scrape down the sides of the bowl, add the remaining ingredients and mix until everything is well incorporated. Scrape down the sides of the bowl and mix again. Cover and refrigerate at least 1 hour and up to 2 days.

Preheat the oven to 350°F.

Drop heaping teaspoons of the dough 2 inches apart onto an ungreased cookie sheet and using your hands, form into crescents. Transfer to the oven and bake until the cookies are just beginning to brown on the edges, about 15 minutes. Transfer the cookies to a wire rack, cool, and then roll in confectioners' sugar. Let the cookie sheet cool completely between batches and repeat with the remaining dough.

Rosemary Walnut Shortbread

YIELD: ABOUT 3 DOZEN COOKIES

Less dense than a classic shortbread, and caramel-y from the dark brown sugar, this sophisticated shortbread has a very subtle rosemary flavor, with chunks of walnuts instead of the more traditional ground nuts. The graham flour adds another dimension of nuttiness. Serve these after dinner with a dessert wine.

Named after Sylvester Graham, graham flour is a type of whole wheat flour (most notably used in graham crackers) made by grinding each piece of the wheat kernel separately, instead of all at once as for regular whole wheat flour. The flavor is infinitely superior to whole wheat flour and can be substituted with great success for part of the white flour in many recipes. I love it! You can buy graham flour at better supermarkets and most whole food stores.

½ cup (¼ pound/1 stick) unsalted butter, at room temperature

½ cup dark brown sugar

½ teaspoon vanilla extract

½ cup walnuts, lightly toasted (see page 10), cooled and coarsely chopped

1½ teaspoons finely chopped fresh rosemary leaves

¾ cup all-purpose white flour

½ cup graham flour

½ teaspoon kosher salt

Place the butter and sugar in the bowl of a mixer fitted with the paddle attachment and mix until smooth and creamy. Scrape down the sides of the bowl, add the vanilla and mix well. Scrape down the sides of the bowl, add the remaining ingredients and mix until everything is well incorporated. Scrape down the sides of the bowl and mix again.

Form into two 1½-inch-diameter logs and cover with parchment paper. Place the logs in a resealable plastic bag and refrigerate for at least 1 hour and up to 2 days, or freeze for up to 2 months.

Preheat the oven to 325°F. Line a cookie sheet with parchment paper.

With the tip of a very sharp knife, cut ⅜-inch slices of the dough and place 2 inches apart on the prepared cookie sheet. Transfer to the oven and bake until the cookies are just beginning to brown on the edges, about 20 minutes. Transfer to a wire rack to cool. Let the cookie sheet cool completely between batches and repeat with the remaining dough.

Toasted Hazelnut Shortbread Cookies

Like all shortbread, these little, dense and buttery cookies are great to serve with fruit and/or tea when you don't want a substantial dessert yet want something sweet.

1 cup (½ pound/2 sticks) unsalted butter, at room temperature

⅓ cup white sugar

¼ cup light brown sugar

1 teaspoon vanilla extract

¾ cup hazelnuts, finely ground lightly toasted (see page 10), and cooled (start with 1 cup whole hazelnuts)

2 cups all-purpose white flour

1 teaspoon kosher salt

¼ cup confectioners' sugar, for sprinkling

Place the butter and white and brown sugars in the bowl of a mixer fitted with the paddle attachment and mix until smooth and creamy. Scrape down the sides of the bowl, add the vanilla and hazelnuts and mix well. Scrape down the sides of the bowl, add the remaining ingredients except the confectioners' sugar and mix until everything is well incorporated. Scrape down the sides of the bowl and mix again. The dough will seem excessively dry, but don't worry—that's the way it's supposed to be.

Form the dough into a ball, cover with plastic wrap and refrigerate for at least ½ hour and up to 2 days.

Preheat the oven to 350°F.

To form the cookies, break off into small pieces and roll into balls. Place 2 inches apart on an ungreased cookie sheet. Transfer to the oven and bake until the edges just begin to brown, 12 to 14 minutes. Cool for 2 minutes, transfer to a wire rack, and sprinkle with the confectioners' sugar. Let the cookie sheet cool completely between batches and repeat with the remaining dough.

Six-Layer Cookies

YIELD: ABOUT 3 DOZEN COOKIES

Inspired by the flavor of six-layer bars (graham cracker crust with layers of chocolate chips, coconut, sweetened condensed milk, nuts and more chocolate chips), these are light and crunchy and I find it almost unbearable to stop eating them. The flavor emerges when they have cooled so it's best to wait. The first time I made them I was rushing to go somewhere and although I had turned the oven off, left them in the oven to cool down. This makes them dry out and get even crunchier, which I love and so now I always follow this unusual method.

½ cup (¼ pound/1 stick) unsalted butter, at room temperature

¾ cup white sugar

¾ cup light brown sugar

2 large eggs, at room temperature

1 cup all-purpose white flour

1 cup graham flour

1 teaspoon kosher salt

¾ teaspoon baking soda

1 cup lightly toasted (see page 83) and cooled sweetened coconut flakes

1 cup (6 ounces) semi-sweet chocolate chips

1 cup pecans, lightly toasted (see page 10), cooled and coarsely chopped

Preheat the oven to 350°F. Line a cookie sheet with parchment paper.

Place the butter and sugars in the bowl of a mixer fitted with the paddle attachment and mix until smooth and creamy. Scrape down the sides of the bowl, add the eggs, one at a time, mixing well between additions. Scrape down the sides of the bowl, add the flours, salt and baking soda and mix until everything is well incorporated. Scrape down the sides of the bowl, add the coconut, chocolate chips and pecans and mix again.

Place heaping teaspoonfuls 2 inches apart on the prepared cookie sheet and transfer to the oven. Bake until the edges begin to firm up, 12 to 14 minutes. For really crispy cookies, turn off the oven and let the cookies cool in the oven. Transfer to a wire rack. Let the cookie sheet cool completely between batches and repeat with the remaining dough.

Cocoa Cookies

I always make these when my nephew Michael is coming over as they are his most beloved of all cookies. Chewy when warm, crispy-crunchy when cool, large, flat and chocolate-y, they can be embellished with toasted nuts, chocolate chips and/or chopped candy canes.

1 cup (½ pound/2 sticks) unsalted butter,
   at room temperature

1 cup white sugar

2 large eggs, at room temperature

1 tablespoon vanilla extract

2 cups all-purpose white flour

1 cup unsweetened cocoa powder

1 teaspoon baking soda

½ teaspoon baking powder

½ teaspoon kosher salt

1½ cups walnuts, pecans or hazelnuts,
   lightly toasted (see page 10), cooled
   and coarsely chopped

Preheat the oven to 350°F. Line a cookie sheet with parchment paper.

Place the butter and sugar in the bowl of a mixer fitted with the paddle attachment and mix until smooth and creamy. Scrape down the sides of the bowl, add the eggs, mixing well between additions. Scrape down the sides of the bowl, add the remaining ingredients and mix until everything is well incorporated. Scrape down the sides of the bowl and mix again.

Place heaping teaspoonfuls of dough 2 inches apart on the prepared cookie sheet and transfer to the oven. Bake until the edges begin to firm up, 12 to 14 minutes; do not overbake. For crispy cookies, let cool on the cookie sheet. Transfer to a wire rack and repeat with the remaining dough. These are also delicious frozen.

Almond Coconut Macaroons

I couldn't decide whether to make an almond macaroon or a coconut macaroon, liking and disliking qualities in both. I decided instead to combine them to include only the qualities I liked best. Here you have the best of both: sweet, nutty and chewy and perfect for people who can't have flour.

¾ cup white sugar

3 cups almonds, lightly toasted (see page 10) and cooled

1½ cups unsweetened dried coconut flakes

4 large egg whites

1 teaspoon vanilla extract

Pinch of kosher salt

Preheat the oven to 350°F. Line a cookie sheet with parchment paper.

Place the sugar, almonds and coconut in the bowl of a food processor fitted with a metal blade and process until the mixture looks like fine sand. Transfer to a large bowl, add the egg whites, vanilla and salt and mix, using a wooden spoon, until everything is well incorporated.

Place heaping teaspoonfuls of the dough 2 inches apart on the prepared cookie sheet. Transfer to the oven and bake until the edges begin to firm up, about 15 minutes. Transfer the cookies to a wire rack. Let the cookie sheet cool completely between batches and repeat with the remaining dough.

Breakfast Cookies

Great for road trips, camping, a meal in itself, a substitute for a power bar or breakfast on the run, these robust and luscious cookies are basically power-packed ingredients bound together by dough. They have more fiber, less sugar and less flour than nearly all other cookies.

Sweet and nutty, flax seeds are small, tough, reddish-brown seeds that are high in omega-3 and good for your heart.

1 cup (½ pound/2 sticks) unsalted butter, at room temperature

½ cup light or dark brown sugar

¼ cup white sugar

2 large eggs, at room temperature

2 teaspoons vanilla extract

1 cup quick-cooking or old-fashioned oats

½ cup plus 2 tablespoons graham flour

½ cup all-purpose white flour

1 teaspoon baking soda

1 teaspoon kosher salt

½ cup Grape Nuts cereal

¼ cup toasted wheat germ

2 tablespoons oat bran

2 tablespoons ground flax seed

½ cup dark raisins or dried cranberries

½ cup chopped dried apricots

½ cup almonds, lightly toasted (see page 10), cooled and coarsely chopped

½ cup walnut halves, lightly toasted (see page 10), cooled and coarsely chopped

½ cup unsweetened dried coconut flakes, lightly toasted (see page 83) and cooled

Preheat the oven to 350°F. Line a cookie sheet with parchment paper.

Place the butter and sugars in the bowl of a mixer fitted with the paddle attachment and mix until smooth and creamy. Scrape down the sides of the bowl, add the eggs, one at a time, and the vanilla, mixing well between additions. Scrape down the sides of the bowl, add the oats, flours, baking soda and salt and mix until everything is well incorporated. Scrape down the sides of the bowl and mix again. Add the remaining ingredients and mix until everything is well incorporated.

To form the cookies: using a large scoop or ¼-cup measure, place balls of dough about 2 inches apart on the prepared cookie sheet. Using your hand or the bottom of a water glass, press down until flattened. Alternatively, you can roll the dough into a log and refrigerate for up to 2 weeks (see page 4).

Transfer to the oven and bake until the cookies begin to brown at the edges, 12 to 15 minutes. Cool on the cookie sheet. Transfer to a wire rack and repeat with the remaining dough.

Lime Zest Cookies

Light and zingy, these buttery, green-flecked shortbread-like cookies are crisp on the edges and dense in the center. I have a weakness for serving (and consuming) them with cranberry and/or mango sorbet.

1 cup (½ pound/2 sticks) unsalted butter,
   at room temperature

¾ cup white sugar

1 large egg, at room temperature

1 teaspoon fresh lime juice

1 teaspoon fresh lime zest

2¼ cups all-purpose white flour

½ teaspoon baking powder

¼ teaspoon kosher salt

Place the butter and sugar in the bowl of a mixer fitted with the paddle attachment and mix until smooth and creamy. Scrape down the sides of the bowl, add the egg, lime juice and lime zest, one at a time, mixing well between additions. Scrape down the sides of the bowl, add the flour, baking powder and salt and mix until everything is well incorporated.

Divide the dough into 3 small balls and place each ball into the center of a large resealable plastic bag. Place each bag on the counter and, using a rolling pin, roll the dough from the center toward the edges until it is ¼ inch thick. Refrigerate for at least 1 hour and up to 2 days. Alternatively, you can roll the dough into a 1-inch log (see page 4).

Preheat the oven to 400°F. Remove 1 sheet of dough from the freezer at a time.

Using a 1-inch round cookie cutter, punch out cookies and place on an ungreased cookie sheet. Transfer to the oven and bake until the cookies are golden brown, 7 to 10 minutes. Cool on the cookie sheet. Transfer to a wire rack and repeat with the remaining dough.

Anise Almond Biscotti

YIELD: ABOUT 4 DOZEN COOKIES

Traditionally flavored with anise seed, these classic Italian cookies are often eaten for breakfast with coffee or hot chocolate and later in the day with wine. Crunchy and hard, they are great for dipping.

Sambuca is an Italian liqueur often used as a flavoring in pastries. Made from elderberries and flavored with anise, sambuca is a popular after-dinner drink that helps bump up the anise flavor in these biscotti.

½ cup (¼ pound/1 stick) unsalted butter,
   at room temperature

1 cup white sugar

2 large eggs, at room temperature

1 tablespoon sambuca

1 cup almonds, lightly toasted (see page 10),
   cooled and roughly chopped

1¾ cups all-purpose white flour

2 teaspoons crushed (not ground) anise seed
   or fennel

¾ teaspoon baking soda

¾ teaspoon baking powder

½ teaspoon kosher salt

Preheat the oven to 350°F. Line a cookie sheet with parchment paper.

Place the butter and sugar in the bowl of a mixer fitted with the paddle attachment and mix until smooth and creamy. Scrape down the sides of the bowl, add the eggs, one at a time, and the sambuca, mixing well between additions. Scrape down the sides of the bowl, add the remaining ingredients and mix until everything is well incorporated. Scrape down the sides of the bowl and mix again until it forms a wet, sticky dough.

Divide the dough in half and form each piece into an 8-inch log. Place the 2 logs as far apart as you can on the prepared cookie sheet and transfer to the oven. Bake until they are just golden and beginning to crack, about 20 minutes. Set aside to cool for about 20 minutes.

Lower the oven temperature to 250°F.

continued on next page

With the tip of a very sharp knife or a serrated knife, cut the logs into ⅜-inch slices on the diagonal and return to the prepared cookie sheet without crowding. Transfer to the oven and bake until the biscotti are just beginning to brown on the edges, about 5 minutes per side, turning once during baking. Transfer to a wire rack to cool. Let the cookie sheet cool completely between batches and repeat with the remaining slices.

Toasted Coconut and Oatmeal Cookies

YIELD: 3 TO 4 DOZEN COOKIES

Although coconut used to get a bad rap for its high saturated fat content, new research shows that not all saturated fat is bad and in fact, eating coconut with some restraint is good for you. In truth, I find its flavor and texture irresistible.

1 cup sweetened coconut flakes

½ cup (¼ pound/1 stick) unsalted butter, at room temperature

½ cup white sugar

½ cup light brown sugar

1 large egg, at room temperature

1 teaspoon vanilla extract

1 cup all-purpose white flour

1 cup quick-cooking or old-fashioned oats, ground to a powder

1 teaspoon baking powder

¼ teaspoon baking soda

½ teaspoon kosher salt

Preheat the oven to 350°F. Line a cookie sheet with parchment paper.

Place the coconut on the prepared cookie sheet, transfer to the oven, and bake until the coconut is just beginning to brown and become fragrant, 7 to 10 minutes. Set aside to cool.

Place the butter and sugars in the bowl of a mixer fitted with the paddle attachment and mix until smooth and creamy. Scrape down the sides of the bowl, add the egg and vanilla, mixing well between additions. Scrape down the sides of the bowl, add the remaining ingredients, including the cooled coconut, and mix until everything is well incorporated. Scrape down the sides of the bowl and mix again.

Drop the dough by heaping teaspoons about 2 inches apart on the prepared cookie sheet. Alternatively, you can roll the dough into a log (see page 4). Transfer to the oven and bake until the cookies begin to brown at the edges, 10 to 12 minutes. Cool on the cookie sheet. Transfer the cookies to a wire rack and repeat with the remaining dough.

cookies

Candy Cane Cookies

At Christmas this past year, we decorated our dining room chandelier with candy canes. Weeks into the New Year, Ben and I were sitting at the table, looked up and decided to do something with those few still remaining. We put them in our food processor and, using another recipe, replaced half the sugar with the ground-up candy canes. Next year, we'll add them to the cookies we bring to friends. If you are feeling especially creative, roll the dough out and cut out candy cane shapes.

1¼ cups (2½ sticks) unsalted butter, at room temperature

½ cup white sugar

½ cup finely crushed candy canes

1 large egg, at room temperature

3 cups all-purpose white flour

½ teaspoon baking powder

½ teaspoon kosher salt

Place the butter, sugar and crushed candy canes in the bowl of a mixer fitted with the paddle attachment and mix until smooth and creamy. Scrape down the sides of the bowl, add the egg and mix well. Scrape down the sides of the bowl, add the remaining ingredients and mix until everything is well incorporated. Scrape down the sides of the bowl and mix again.

Form into 1½-inch-diameter logs and cover with parchment paper. Place the logs in a resealable plastic bag and refrigerate for at least 1 hour and up 2 days or freeze for up to 2 months.

Preheat the oven to 375°F. Line a cookie sheet with parchment paper.

With the tip of a very sharp knife, cut ¼- to ½-inch slices of the dough and place on the prepared pan. Transfer to the oven and bake until the cookies are just beginning to brown on the edges, 12 to 14 minutes. Transfer to a wire rack to cool. Let the cookie sheet cool completely between batches and repeat with the remaining dough.

list of recipe titles
by the week

WEEK 1:   Gingersnaps........ *page 2*

WEEK 2:   Ben's Molasses Cookies........ *page 5*

WEEK 3:   Amanda Hewell's Coffee Crisps........ *page 6*

WEEK 4:   Chocolate Chip Oatmeal Cookies........ *page 8*

WEEK 5:   Banana Nut Cookies........ *page 9*

WEEK 6:   Sandra Fairbank's Tiny Poppy Seed Cookies........ *page 11*

WEEK 7:   Pecan Sandies........ *page 14*

WEEK 8:   German Chocolate Cookies........ *page 16*

WEEK 9:   White Chocolate and Dried
Cranberry Cookies........ *page 18*

WEEK 10:   Toasted Cashew and Orange Cookies........ *page 20*

WEEK 11:   Mary Granfield's Chocolate Walnut Cookies........ *page 21*

WEEK 12:   Pecan Shorties........ *page 22*

Cookies

WEEK 13: Chai Shortbread........ *page* 23

WEEK 14: Paige Retus's Fudge-Topped
Toffee Cookies........ *page* 24

WEEK 15: Espresso Shortbread........ *page* 26

WEEK 16: Vanilla Bean Sugar Cookies........ *page* 28

WEEK 17: Chocolate Raisin Walnut
Oatmeal Cookies........ *page* 30

WEEK 18: Spicy Cocoa Cookies........ *page* 32

WEEK 19: Orange Almond Cookies........ *page* 35

WEEK 20: Jenny deBell's Snickerdoodles........ *page* 36

WEEK 21: Brown Sugar Cookies........ *page* 37

WEEK 22: Pogasca........ *page* 38

WEEK 23: Cream Cheese Cookies........ *page* 40

WEEK 24: Date Nut Cookies........ *page 41*

WEEK 25: Jeff Conti's Peanut Butter "Cookies"........ *page 42*

WEEK 26: Savory Cheese Cookies........ *page 43*

WEEK 27: Cornmeal Shortbread and Jam Tots........ *page 44*

WEEK 28: Irish Lace Cookies........ *page 46*

WEEK 29: Chewy Molasses Cookies........ *page 48*

WEEK 30: Olive Oil and Wine Cookies........ *page 49*

WEEK 31: Annie Fischel's Meringues........ *page 50*

WEEK 32: Celina Windzio's Nantucket Peanut Butter Cookies........ *page 52*

WEEK 33: Nancy Olin's Chocolate Chip Cookies........ *page 54*

WEEK 34: Sharon Smith's Spice Cookies........ *page 56*

WEEK 35: Crispy Chocolate Chip Cookies........ *page 57*

WEEK 36: Cocoa Toffee Chunk Cookies........ *page 58*

WEEK 37: Black Chocolate Oatmeal Cookies........ *page 60*

WEEK 38: Citrus Shortbread........ *page 61*

WEEK 39: Mexican Wedding Cookies........ *page 62*

WEEK 40: Agnes Wazenski's Applesauce
Butterscotch Cookies........ *page 64*

WEEK 41: Almond Butter Oat Cookies........ *page 65*

WEEK 42: Almond Crescents........ *page 66*

WEEK 43: Rosemary Walnut Shortbread........ *page 68*

WEEK 44: Toasted Hazelnut Shortbread Cookies........ *page 70*

WEEK 45: Six-Layer Cookies........ *page 71*

WEEK 46: Cocoa Cookies........ *page 72*

WEEK 47: Almond Coconut Macaroons........ *page 74*

WEEK 48: **Breakfast Cookies**........ *page* 76

WEEK 49: **Lime Zest Cookies**........ *page* 78

WEEK 50: **Anise Almond Biscotti**........ *page* 80

WEEK 51: **Toasted Coconut and Oatmeal**........ *page* 83

WEEK 52: **Candy Cane Cookies**........ *page* 84

Index

A

Agnes Wazenski's Applesauce
   Butterscotch Cookies, 64
Almond Anise Biscotti, 80–82
Almond Butter Oat Cookies, 65
Almond Cookies:
   Coconut Macaroons, 74–75
   Crescents, 66–67
   Orange, 35
Amanda Hewell's Coffee
   Crisps, 6–7
Anise Almond Biscotti, 80–82
Annie Fischel's Meringues,
   50–51
Applesauce Butterscotch
   Cookies, Agnes Wazenski's,
   64

B

Banana Nut Cookies, 9
Ben's Molasses Cookies, 5
Biscotti, Anise Almond, 80–82
Black Chocolate Oatmeal
   Cookies, 60
Breakfast Cookies, 76–77
Brown Sugar Cookies, 37

Butterscotch Applesauce
   Cookies, Agnes Wazenski's,
   64

C

Candy Cane Cookies, 84–85
Cashew, Toasted, and Orange
   Cookies, 20
Celina Windzio's Nantucket
   Peanut Butter Cookies,
   52–53
Chai Shortbread, 23
Cheese Cookies, Savory, 43
Chewy Molasses Cookies, 48
Chocolate Chip Cookies:
   Crispy, 57
   Nancy Olin's, 54–55
   Oatmeal, 8
Chocolate Cookies:
   Black Chocolate Oatmeal,
      60
   German Chocolate, 16–17
   Raisin Walnut Oatmeal,
      30–31
   Walnut, Mary Granfield's, 21
   White Chocolate and Dried

Cranberry, 18–19
Citrus Shortbread, 61
Cocoa Cookies, 72–73
   Spicy, 32–34
   Toffee Chunk, 58–59
Coconut, Toasted, and
   Oatmeal Cookies, 83
Coconut Almond Macaroons,
   74–75
Coffee Crisps, Amanda
   Hewell's, 6–7
cookie logs, 4
Cornmeal Shortbread and Jam
   Tots, 44–45
Cranberry, Dried, and White
   Chocolate Cookies, 18–19
Cream Cheese Cookies, 40
Crispy Chocolate Chip
   Cookies, 57

D

Date Nut Cookies, 41
Dried Cranberry and White
   Chocolate Cookies, 18–19

E

equipment, xiii
Espresso Shortbread, 26–27

F

Fudge-Topped Toffee Cookies,
    Paige Retus's, 24–25

G

German Chocolate Cookies,
    16–17
Gingersnaps, 2–3

H

Hazelnut, Toasted, Shortbread
    Cookies, 70

I

ingredients, xii
Irish Lace Cookies, 46–47

J

Jeff Conti's Peanut Butter
    "Cookies," 42
Jenny deBell's Snickerdoodles,
    36

L

Lime Zest Cookies, 78–79
logs, cookie, 4

M

Macaroons, Almond Coconut,
    74–75
Mary Granfield's Chocolate
    Walnut Cookies, 21
Meringues, Annie Fischel's,
    50–51
Mexican Wedding Cookies,
    62–63
Molasses Cookies:
    Ben's, 5
    Chewy, 48

N

Nancy Olin's Chocolate Chip
    Cookies, 54–55
Nantucket Peanut Butter
    Cookies, Celina Windzio's,
    52–53
nuts:
    Almond Anise Biscotti,
        80–82
    Almond Butter Oat Cookies,
        65
    Almond Coconut
        Macaroons, 74–75

Almond Crescents, 66–67
Almond Orange Cookies, 35
Banana Nut Cookies, 9
Cashew, Toasted, and
    Orange Cookies, 20
Date Nut Cookies, 41
Hazelnut, Toasted,
    Shortbread Cookies, 70
Pecan Sandies, 14–15
Pecan Shorties, 22
toasting, 10
Walnut Chocolate Cookies,
    Mary Granfield's, 21
Walnut Chocolate Raisin
    Oatmeal Cookies, 30–31
Walnut Rosemary
    Shortbread, 68–69

O

Oat Almond Butter Cookies, 65
Oatmeal Cookies:
    Black Chocolate, 60
    Chocolate Chip, 8
    Chocolate Raisin Walnut,
        30–31
    and Toasted Coconut, 83
Olive Oil and Wine Cookies,
    49
Orange Cookies:
    Almond, 35
    and Toasted Cashew, 20

P

Paige Retus's Fudge-Topped
  Toffee Cookies, 24–25
Peanut Butter Cookies:
  Celina Windzio's Nantucket,
    52–53
  Jeff Conti's, 42
Pecan Sandies, 14–15
Pecan Shorties, 22
Pogasca, 38–39
Poppy Seed Cookies, Sandra
  Fairbank's Tiny, 11–13

R

Raisin Chocolate Walnut
  Oatmeal Cookies, 30–31
Rosemary Walnut Shortbread,
  68–69

S

Sandra Fairbank's Tiny Poppy
  Seed Cookies, 11–13
Savory Cheese Cookies, 43
Sharon Smith's Spice Cookies,
  56

Shortbread:
  Chai, 23
  Citrus, 61
  Cornmeal, and Jam Tots,
    44–45
  Espresso, 26–27
  Rosemary Walnut, 68–69
  Toasted Hazelnut Cookies,
    70
Six-Layer Cookies, 71
Snickerdoodles, Jenny deBell's,
  36
Spice Cookies, Sharon Smith's,
  56
Spicy Cocoa Cookies, 32–34
Sugar Cookies:
  Brown Sugar, 37
  Vanilla Bean, 28–29

T

Toasted Cashew and Orange
  Cookies, 20
Toasted Coconut and Oatmeal
  Cookies, 83
Toasted Hazelnut Shortbread
  Cookies, 70
toasting nuts, 10

Toffee Chunk Cocoa Cookies,
  58–59
Toffee Cookies, Fudge-Topped,
  Paige Retus's, 24–25

V

Vanilla Bean Sugar Cookies,
  28–29

W

Walnut Chocolate Cookies:
  Mary Granfield's, 21
  Raisin Oatmeal, 30–31
Walnut Rosemary Shortbread,
  68–69
Wedding Cookies, Mexican,
  62–63
White Chocolate and Dried
  Cranberry Cookies, 18–19
Wine and Olive Oil Cookies,
  49